better together

This book is best read together, grownup and kid.

a kids book about™

a kids book about™ GOD

by Paul J. Pastor

a
kids
book
about™

Printed in the United States of America

Library of Congress cataloging available.

A Kids Book About books are exclusively available online
on the A Kids Book About website.

To share your stories, ask questions, or inquire about bulk
purchases (schools, libraries, and nonprofits), please use
the following email address:

hello@akidsbookabout.com

www.akidsbookabout.com

ISBN: 978-1-951253-43-1

For Elaia, Emmaus, and Markos Arcturus Pastor.

I love you.

- Dad

Intro

An old saying tells us we shouldn't discuss religion in polite company. When it comes to kids, the old saying is wrong.

Kids are naturally curious about the biggest human ideas. Both as a parent and someone who works at the intersections of theology and culture, I often see the difference between the honest, free way that kids discuss matters of the soul and the many complications that we bring to spirituality as we age.

There's another saying I heard from a friend once: people don't find harmony by going *around* their true beliefs, but by going *through* them. I don't know what you do or don't believe about God. What I hope to do in this short book is simply help start a conversation, one not focused on finding all the perfect answers, but on seeking the really good questions. Will you join me?

Hi, I'm Paul.

I'm a pretty ordinary guy.

Like a lot of people,
I believe in God.

But talking about God
isn't always easy.

I mean, how do you talk
about something as
big and wild as...

OD

Do you start by
closing your eyes
and saying a prayer?

Do you start by
looking up at the sky?

Do you start by
jumping up and down
on one leg and touching
your nose?

(You might want to try that just in case.)

Talking about God is difficult because everyone seems to have **different ideas** about God.

Some people don't think God is real.

For other people, it seems like God is the only thing they talk about!

And some people are just sort of shruggy and in-between, like they would rather go to the dentist **than talk about God.**

WHAT'S
WITH

UP THAT?

No matter what we believe, shouldn't **we talk about God?**

What do you think?

No really—**what do you think?**

Talk about it with the person reading this book!

OK then...

What is the point of
this book anyway?

The point of this book **is not** to give you all the answers.

Answers can be for another time.

I don't even have all the questions about God.

The point of this book is to get us...

talki
talk
tak
t

Because I think God is
SUPER IMPORTANT
for kids and grownups
to talk about.

SO LET'S TALK.

"GOD"

What do you think of when you hear that word?

A big-bearded old man in the sky?

A crazy giant carrying thunderbolts around and smiting stuff?

Mother Earth?

A flying spaghetti monster?

Or a great big Nothing?

(It's also OK if you don't think of anything at all.)

You might think of
100 different things.

But you also
probably have
some questions.

GREAT!

Because right now I want us to talk, and talking starts best with **questions**.

Now you're big enough
to know that questions
about God can be

**big or little,
serious or silly,
long or short.**

The important thing is
to just ask questions.

**The ones you're
really wondering.**

So **let's practice** this for a minute.

Maybe you're wondering...

Who made the world?

Who made me?

Why do bad things happen?

Like, REALLY BAD THINGS?

Is God even real?

If God is real, is God good?

Does God care about me?

What happens when things die?

Does God have hair?

Who made God?

How can I live a good life?

Is God watching me?

ALL the time?

Even when I ... (poop)?

Who knows what is really true?

Does God laugh?

Does God cry?

Does God ever take a vacation?

Why doesn't God stop bad stuff?

Why do some people say God
has so many rules?

Why can't I see God?

Woah.
Some of those are silly!
And some of them
are pretty tough.

But they're real!

OK, what is one thing you wonder **RIGHT NOW** about God?

*Hey grownup, don't forget to really
listen when kids ask questions!

Grownup, have you ever really wondered anything about God?

*Hey kid, your turn to listen for a quick minute!

Wow,
those are good questions.
**And hey, look
what's just happened!**

All of a sudden you're talking about **the Really Big Questions of Life.**

This is why it's so important that...

WE TALK ABOUT GOD.

Because when we do,
we start connecting.

We **start really seeing**
the world and each other.

We can take what's inside us
and **talk about it** a little more.

But sometimes we end up arguing about God.

If I say there is one God, someone somewhere will think:

"No, there are lots of gods!"

If I say that God cares about us, someone somewhere will say:

"God doesn't care! God has left us all alone here."

If I say that we can really know God—like we would know another person—someone somewhere will say:

"We can't know God! God is too different from us."

If I say that God is real, someone somewhere will say:

"There is no God, there's only nature!"

The arguments about God could go on and on.

They **HAVE** gone on and on.

For thousands of years.

And this isn't necessarily bad

What's bad is when we're mean
to each other or try and hurt
one another because we
don't agree about God.

And do you know why
this is bad?

Because I believe...

GOD IS LOVE.

(By the way, I didn't come up with that.)

And the exact millisecond
that we stop loving,

no matter **WHAT** we believe,

or how good we are at following
the rules, or how much we pray,

or **WHATEVER,**
we are beginning to miss the
point completely.

I believe it is through
real love that we know God.

So even though there are a **BUNCH** of things that I believe about God in my head, and all of those things matter a lot...

What's most important is what's happening in my heart.

THE TRUTH IS...

none of us are perfect.

And the love of the God
I believe in is always
welcoming, always strong,
and always knows what
I need to grow in my love.

So whether or not you believe in a different God or no God at all,

Whether you change your mind a couple (or 1,000,000) times about what you think or believe,

Whether your ideas make you happy or sad or confused...

LEARNING TO KNOW GOD IS A JOURNEY.

You get to ask **questions**.

You get to **wonder**.

You get to **have fun**.

You get to **think**.

You get to pray and sing and play and dance and paint out your thoughts and **feelings about God.**

SO.

Let's keep **talking**.

Keep **asking** questions.

Keep **wondering** and **loving** what is true.

Because you know something?

I don't think we'll ever have to stop.

Outro

As you close this book, I invite you to return to the fresh curiosity, honesty, and freedom that children manifest in matters of the spirit. Learn from the kids in your life. Be a little more like them.

And also consider joining me in trying to say more about God rather than less. Be humble and honest of course, and never overbearing. But don't hold back what you really believe! If you do, you will be quietly teaching your kid that either these conversations don't really matter or they're scary. Neither of those postures encourage a rich spiritual life.

Let's wonder together. Let's ask the big questions, and seek the truth, and knock on the door of our own hearts. Let's be open to the love and strength of the great Spirit of Life, who is not far from any one of us, and in whom we live and move and have our being.

God bless you.

find more kids books about

emotions, empathy, optimism, change, belonging, death, feminism, mindfulness, voting, racism, and money.

■ akidsbookabout.com

share your read

Tell somebody, post a photo, or give this book away to share what you care about.